PHONICS CHAPTER BOOKS

A Lot of Hats

by John Shefelbine
Illustrated by Tony Griego

Scholastic Inc.
New York Toronto London Auckland Sydney

Copyright © 1998 by Scholastic Inc.
Scholastic *Phonics Chapter Books* is a trademark of Scholastic Inc.
All rights reserved. Published by Scholastic Inc.
Printed in the U.S.A.
ISBN 0-590-11658-4
4 5 6 7 8 9 10   23   04 03 02 01 00 99 98 97

Dear Teacher/Family Member,

Research has shown that phonics is an essential strategy for figuring out unknown words. Early readers need the opportunity to learn letter sounds and how to blend or put them together to make words. These skills must be practiced over and over again by reading stories containing words with the sounds being taught.

That's why I'm happy to be an author and Program Coordinator of the **Phonics Chapter Books**. These books provide early readers with playful, fanciful stories in easy-to-manage chapters. More importantly, the words in the stories are controlled for phonics sounds and common sight words. Once sounds and sight words have been introduced, they are continually reviewed and applied in succeeding stories, so children will be able to decode these books—and read them on their own. There is nothing more powerful and encouraging than success.

John Shefelbine
Associate Professor, Reading Education
California State University, Sacramento

1 The Hats

Tom and Mom and Dad sat.

Mom said, "I can see a lot of hats.
Can you see the hats?"

CONTENTS

Tom said, "I can.
A hat is on the mat."

Dad said, "I see hats.
Can you see 3 hats?"

Tom said, "I can see 2 hats.
I can see a hat on the man
and the hat on top of the mat."

Dad said, "I see the hat on the mat and the hat on the man. I can see a hat on the mop."

Mom said, "I see 4 hats! I see hats on the mop, on the man, and on the mat. And I see a hat on Dad!"

2 1, 2, 3.
Who Is It?

Dad said, "Who is it?"

Tom said, "I am it.
1, 2, 3, 4, 5, 6, 7, 8, 9, 10."

Mom and Dad hid.

Tom said, "I see Mom.
1, 2, 3. Mom is it!"

"I am it," said Mom.

Tom and Dad hid.

"1, 2, 3. I see Dad.
Dad is it," Mom said.

Dad said, "Can you see my hat?
Who hid my hat?"

"I am sad," said Dad.
Dad sat on the mat.

Mom said, "I see the hat.
Look at the mat!"

Dad sat on the mat on the hat.
"I see my hat!" said Dad.

Tom said, "1, 2, 3. The hat is it!"

3 The Map

Tom and Ann sat on a log.
Tom had a map, a pot, and a mop.

Tom said, "Look at the map on
my lap. Can you see the <u>X</u>?
The <u>X</u> is on the hill."

Tom and Ann looked at the hill.

Tom said, "Ann, look at the mat.
You and I can hop on the mat!"

Ann said, "I like to hop."

Tom said, "I like to hop and hop."

Tom hit his pot. Tap!
The pot hit his mop. Tap! Tap!
The mop hit Tom. Tap! Pat! Tap!

Ann said, "I can hop.
You can stop."

4 The Fan Hat

Tom and Ann like to look.

Tom said, "Look! I see 3 fans.
I like fans. I like them if I am hot.
Can you see them?"

Ann said, "I see the fans.
Can you see the hat?"

Tom said, "I can see it.
I like the hat."

Ann said, "Will it fit?
Will the hat fit?"

Tom said, "The hat fits.
I like it a lot, but I am hot.
Can you fan me, Ann?"

Ann said, "Tom, look!
Look at the fan on the hat!"

5 ⭐ Who Is He?

Ann said, "Look at the man.
Who is he?"

Tom said, "He looks like my dad."

"Look at his pot and his pan,"
said Ann. "He has a mitt.
The pan looks hot."

Tom said, "Can you see his hat?
He is not my dad, but who is he?"

Mom said, "Who is it?
Who can you see?"

Ann said, "It is a man. He has a hat."

Tom said, "He has a pan
and a pot. He looks like Dad,
but it is not Dad."

"Who is the man?" said Mom.

Dad said, "The man is my dad."

 6 The Cat Nap

Tom has a cat.
Ann has a cat.

Ann's cat is Mat Cat.
Mat Cat likes to nap on a mat.

Tom's cat is Lap Cat.
Lap Cat likes to nap on Tom's lap.

Mom said, "Tom, I see you and
I see Ann, but where is the cat?"

Tom and Ann looked and looked.

Mom said, "I do not see the cat.
Where is he? Where is Lap Cat?"

Ann said, "Tom, do you see Lap Cat?
Look on the mat."

Tom said, "My cat is not on the mat.
Lap Cat likes to nap on my lap,
but Lap Cat is not on my lap.
Where is he?"

Ann said, "I do not see Lap Cat
on the fan. I do not see him."

Tom said, "I see him! Look at my cap.
Lap Cat likes to nap on my lap
and in my cap!"

Bill and Tom at Bat

7

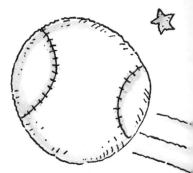

Tom said, "I am Tom. Who are you?"

Bill said, "I am Bill. Do you like to bat? Do you like to hit the ball? Look. I can hit it."

BAM! Bill hit the ball.

Tom said, "I can't do it. I can't hit the ball. I do not like to bat."

Bill said, "You can do it. You can bat. Look at the ball and hit it."

BAM! Tom hit the ball.

"I hit it!" said Tom.
"I can do it. I like to bat."

BAM!

21

Who Will Win?

Tom said, "Where is my Lap Cat?
Where is Mat Cat?"

Ann said, "I can see them.
The cats are on the hill.
Mat Cat! Lap Cat!"

Cats are fast.

Tom said, "Lap Cat is fast.
My cat will win."

Ann said, "Why can't my cat win?
Mat Cat is a fast cat. My cat can win."

Tom said, "You can win, Lap Cat!"

Ann said, "But Mat Cat likes her ball.
Mat Cat! Can you see the ball?"

Mat Cat looked at her ball.
Ann said, "Mat Cat wins!"

9 Ants Like Jam

Tom and Ann like picnics.
They like to jog to the hill and sit
on a log.

Ann said, "What's in this?"

Tom said, "Look, Ann.
Look in and see."

"Do I see jam?" said Ann.
"I like jam."

Tom said, "It is jam, lots and
lots of jam."

The ants looked at the jam.
Ants like jam.
Tom looked at the ants.

"What's this?" said Tom.
"Lots and lots of ants!
They like my jam, but I do not
like them."

Ann said, "Tom! Zip the jam up!
Jog as fast as you can!"

10 Dot the Dog

Ann has a cat and a dog.

The cat's name is Mat Cat.

The dog's name is Lad.

Tom has a cat, and Tom likes dogs.

"Did you see the dogs?" Tom said to his dad. "Can we have a dog?"

Tom, Ann, Mom, and Dad looked at
the dogs.

"I do not see a dog like Lad,"
Ann said.

Tom had a little dog in his hand.
"I like this little dog," he said.

"The little dog likes you,"
Mom said.

"OK," Dad said. "You can have
the little dog."

Tom said, "What can we name it?
What's a dog name?
Jill, Jim, Fizz, Bob, Dill, Dip,
Sip, Zip, Zap, Tim, Top, Sam?"

Mom said, "The dog has dots.
We can name her Dot."

Tom said, "I like the name Dot.
I have a dog. Her name is Dot.
Ann has a dog. His name is Lad.
We have 2 cats and 2 dogs!"

11 They Ran and Hid

Dogs do not like cats.
Cats do not like dogs.

Tom and Ann ran to the hill.
The dogs ran to the cats.
The cats ran and hid.

Tom and Ann looked at the dogs.

"Bad dogs!" Ann said.
"We like Mat Cat and Lap Cat."

The dogs ran.

Dad said, "Tom, will you look for
my hat?"

"Who has Dad's hat?" said Tom.
"Lap Cat, did you nap in Dad's hat?"

Lap Cat ran and hid.

"Dot, did you do it?" Tom said.

Yes, she did! She hid Dad's hat.
The hat had a rip in it.

Dad said, "Why did she do this?"
Dot ran and hid.

Tom said, "Dogs! What a job!"

PHONICS

Decodable Words With the Phonic Elements

1 **Hh** hat
hats
-ad Dad
-an man

2 **Ii** it
-id hid

3 **Pp** pat
pot
hop
lap
map
mop
stop
tap
-og log

4 **Ff** fan
fans
fit
fits
if

5 **Nn** not
Ann
man
pan

6 **Cc** cap
cat

7 **Bb** bam
bat
-ill Bill

8 **Ww** will
win
wins

9 **Jj** jam
jog
Zz zip

10 **Dd** Dad
did
Dill
Dip
dog
dogs
Dot
dots
hand
Lad
-op Top

11 **Rr** ran
rip
-ob job